Magical Moments

Mysterious Meetings

Mark D'Albi

Front Cover: Sunset at the lake at Aum Pranava Ashram, Ilanji, India. It shows a mysterious yellow light

Back Cover: Two trees, one intertwined around the other, in Eco Park, Courtallam, India

Amazingly the same feature is repeated five metres away.

ISBN: 9781098839505

Magical Moments Mysterious Meetings

Introduction

This is my humble attempt to give faith to those searching for a spiritual dimension to life and to show the reality of the unseen, spiritual world. I will recount how the spiritual world interacts with our everyday world.

You will read about the myriad ways the spiritual dimension can touch us through the Grace of God, His divine agents the Avatars, Saints and Masters, the blessings of angels and of our friends who are living in the subtle planes.

I will not focus on opinions or theory. Teachings and theory can be found a plenty in our world. Practice is important if one wishes to progress and gain more Light along the Path.

My Guru, Sri Sathya Sai Baba summed up the spiritual Path in His inimitable way as “Love all serve all” and “Help ever hurt ever”.

I hope this guidance resonates with you, because simply putting these two teachings into practice brings us a peace and joy that is immeasurable and will open the door to your own magical moments and mysterious meetings.

You will enjoy this book if you are open to the idea of us receiving help from our friends who are now living the Greater Life, or in heaven if you want to use the term. Our existence here is very limited and circumscribed and many of those who have passed on to the next world actively help us out of compassion. Some of those who help us are the great Angels and Masters, responsible for great healings and miracles.

There are other events I have written about which seem to point to the very fabric of life being able to reflect back to us in a meaningful way. It is as if *all is consciousness* and due to the intensity of emotion, an experience comes back to us as a mirror. That is all the theory you will find. The rest of the book is a light easy read focusing on experiences I had.

It might be easy to dismiss one or two strange and unexplainable events, but when they occur over and over again across a whole life, then one has to admit it is proof enough for the person concerned. The accounts here may stretch your credulity, but I can only confirm that everything happened to me exactly as described.

Apart from the example below, I have omitted all my purely personal and subjective experiences, which number thousands. Such as blissful meditations; spiritual at-one-ments; telepathy; seeing events before they happen and that between myself and my ever-loving, ever-patient teacher, Sathya Sai Baba.

First Transformation

When I was 18, I became very confused and depressed. I was isolated and did not know how to relate to life or people anymore. I was lost and totally angst ridden.

One evening while I was alone at home, something moved me from within and I spontaneously started to cry out to God. And not just quietly, but wailing, crying out loudly for God to help me. This acute anguish lasted for some ten minutes.

But as I sobbed, I felt an unexpected inexplicable Presence around me, a stillness and a clearness, as if I was being protected and embraced.

And then when the tears ceased, I felt an overwhelmingly comforting peace which grew to a supernal Joy. I had never had these feelings before. I had never even prayed before, nor had any religious interest.

But now I knew, stunningly and suddenly, that God LOVES ME. He loved me with so much intensity and depth, with total acceptance and intimacy. I was His, fully healed and embraced.

I underwent a total transformation after this overwhelming miraculous healing. From those powerfully magical moments onwards, I focused on praying, meditating and attempting to move closer to the divine loving Presence I had felt that evening.

I am happy to write that in some measure, this awareness of the Divine has stayed with me every day of my life since then, and has been powerfully and eternally revealed in my Guru, Sri Sathya Sai Baba. This book is not about my decade's long relationship with Him, but I recount a few instances here and there.

My contact with the subtle dimensions has been centred around profound joy, peace, love and bliss. I often bubble over laughing, with a sense of total and complete fulfilment. On countless occasions I have been blessed with transcendent feelings of bliss. As these are purely subjective and personal, I have left them out of this account.

In these true recollections, I have focussed on tangible events that were cognisant through my five senses; or through personal meetings with special people, who may well have been Angels or Masters in disguise or their messengers.

I hope these *magical moments* and *mysterious meetings* will inspire you and give you faith along your path. I have also written these memoirs as a way of affirming and showing gratitude for all the help sent my way, as I know I have caused my friends some extra duties!

Magical Moments

A Moving Light

On the evening that I was to leave my parents' London home at 19 years of age and go and join a volunteer project, I was looking out of my window at the clear night sky.

Suddenly a star-like light appeared and moved fast in a tight arc across the heavens and then disappeared. I have always taken it as a sign of benediction from the Masters, on the night that I entered the adult world.

Shapes in the Sky

I am sure some will find this hard to believe. This occurred a kilometre from the Whitefield, Bangalore residence of Sathya Sai Baba, sometime in 2003. I was walking across a field late afternoon and then looked up at the burgeoning sunset in front of me.

I was stunned to see an amazing collection of six or seven clouds of different *geometric shapes*, even shapes within shapes, such as a red triangle in a green square! These were of large size, proportionate, properly formed, each having their own colour, and not just randomly assorted.

It was as if an intelligence had painted them in the sky. I was totally flabbergasted. Later a French friend confirmed seeing this amazing display.

Potent Omen

On the same subject of clouds, Sai Baba would travel to a hill station called Kodai Kanal every year around April. Many people would follow Him there and I was travelling in a car with a very nice Iranian family. As we approached the hills we stopped for a break and looked ahead to see a very clear Om shaped cloud (in Indian script) above the hills where Sai Baba was staying.

The cloud OM depicted by the 3 figure

This Cloud Will Pass

Yet another cloudy event happened in India. I had been thinking wistfully about visiting the UK.

Then I looked up and saw an exact formation of the British Isles made from clouds. It was not just a vague likeness, but the correct outline in detail. Well my wish to return to UK did pass, just like that cloud.

A Blessing in the Clouds

I had finished a two-week stint as a volunteer with other young people helping in a village in the Czech countryside that had been devastated by a flood. It had been a time of camaraderie, fun and international friendships. I was waiting for my flight home, laying down peacefully on the grass in a small park in Prague. As I looked up, I saw the face of Sai Baba made from clouds. It was an exact image and stayed a couple of minutes. I felt His wonderful Blessing as well.

Running Fish

This miraculous event happened in the backwaters of Kerala, India, near Varkala. I had met two English women and we had hired a boat for sightseeing, something that many tourists do. We had motored up the river, had our lunch and were returning back when something truly extraordinary happened.

While looking ahead watching the wildlife, suddenly two large fish jumped out of the water 'standing up' vertically on their fins and proceeded to run vertically on their back fins from one side of the river to the other!

It all passed off in two or three seconds as they quickly 'ran' across our path, making a splashing noise as they went, then disappearing into the water after traversing about 20 metres!

We were transfixed to the spot and could not believe our eyes. I felt a strange ecstasy watching them that I could not explain. I have checked on the internet and there is nothing about this phenomenon.

Orange Highlight

One day I was reading a book called *Esoteric Healing,* by Alice A. Bailey. She wrote down what she heard telepathically from her Master. He was a Llama called Djwhal Khul, resident in Tibet.

By way of this telepathic communication she contributed over 30 books, which are very respected worldwide. They are a font of knowledge and when I was in my 20's I eagerly devoured them.

One afternoon, as I was reading it, the title of the book on the top of the page suddenly became highlighted in bright orange light, just as if you had drawn across it with an orange highlighter pen. This light remained about 5 seconds, long enough for me to be sure I was not imagining it.

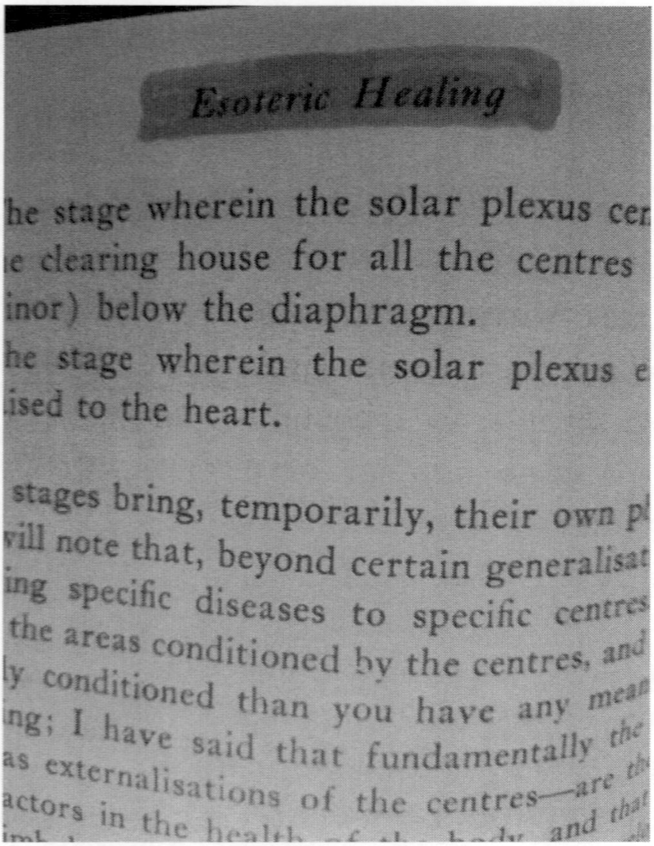

Esoteric Healing

he stage wherein the solar plexus cer
e clearing house for all the centres
inor) below the diaphragm.
he stage wherein the solar plexus e
ised to the heart.

stages bring, temporarily, their own p
vill note that, beyond certain generalisat
ing specific diseases to specific centres
the areas conditioned by the centres, and
ly conditioned than you have any mea
ng; I have said that fundamentally the
as externalisations of the centres—are th
actors in the health of the body, and that

The orange highlight drawn by myself, to show how it looked

Seeing Your Light

It's very rare to see your own aura. But now and again it happens. One day I was in the shower and suddenly for a couple of seconds I could see my aura. I was feeling a bit down at the time, but this sight really cheered me up. If we could see our light and other's too it would make us very happy indeed.

Another time I had just come indoors from outside after some exercise and bent down to take my shoes off. Then in the subdued lighting I clearly saw a blue light covering my right hand. It was a little like a network and was luminescent.

On other occasions in my 20's, as I would be writing in my room, I would often see rays of pink, due to the white paper acting as a clear background. They were a part of my aura.

Classical Colours

Once in my 20's, I went to an open-air classical concert in Kenwood Park, London. There is a proper open style concert hall and a lovely field to sit in, with capacity for about 5,000 people. There I could see the music as colour, emanating from the musicians and their instruments.

Bike-less

One day I was feeling quite happy and then a strong thought came into my mind, from nowhere: *"You won't be so happy when your bike gets stolen."*

Wow - just like that out of the blue. I had never had this thought before. I was quite shocked and found this so disconcerting that I began to keep my bicycle in my flat rather than leave it in the back garden as normal. I did this for two days and then I went on a trip somewhere and left it outside at a rail station locked up. When I returned, you guessed it, it had been stolen!

Well that taught me a lesson - that some things are meant to happen. This helped me feel not so bad about the loss.

Book Appearance

Many years ago, I had been reading a well-known spiritual author, Nisagadatta Maharaj, who I really liked. I wanted to read another of his many books and went to a private spiritual library in London.

I searched for the author, found a book by him and took it to the librarian. He looked a little surprised as he did not recognise it and also did not find any library ticket inside the book, or that it was even registered with the library!

I like to think that the book was placed there for me by an angelic well-wisher.

Needy Knee

Some years ago, I somehow had strained my knee and it was so bad that I could not sit cross legged for meditation. I was quite sad about this, as meditating cross legged was important to me. I had to sit on chairs at meetings and at home, when normally I would be on the floor and I was trying to get used to it.

At the time my friend Klaus and I were running a meditation group. Klaus would lead with some of his inspiring spiritual songs and I would then conduct the Light Meditation, as composed by Sai Baba.

So, we were singing away in the first part of the group and I was sitting on a chair. Somehow the energy became heightened and I was transported into intense bliss, which I could feel all over my body. This deep feeling lasted quite a while and I was feeling radiant.

After the meeting, I noticed that my knee strain was completely and instantly healed. I could even sit down cross legged again and it has stayed that way ever since!

Grasshopper Message

For those with faith, messages come from the unseen world, from angels and Masters and they can be deciphered in meaningful ways. You just need to keep your eyes and ears open.

I had been working as an agency nurse for some months. But I was wondering about getting a permanent job on a ward. I asked my Guru for guidance on this matter and it came in a wonderful way.

One night in October I was returning from a late shift and I was on the second floor of a bus. There were not many people with me and suddenly I saw a grasshopper walking on the back of the seat in front of me.

I was fascinated as I love insects and a grasshopper is very beautiful. It was also quite unusual as the windows were shut as the heating was on - so where had he come from?

He carried on slowly walking in front of me and then proceeded across the top of the chair in front of me. After ten minutes fun of watching him, I thought I should take him outside, so I contrived to get him on my hand, but then he jumped off somewhere – as grasshoppers do! And then it was time for me to get off the bus.

Well that was a Friday and my next shift was on Monday, and unusually I went back to the same ward. I went back to the room where I had to look after the patient and there on the wall, I noticed something I had not seen on my last visit.

A giant blown up picture of a grasshopper! I could not believe it. The message was loud and clear. In Germany agency nurses are known as springers or jumpers. So, I stayed as an agency nurse another year, jumping from one hospital to the next.

Accommodation Receipt Materialisation

Now why I write materialisation will become clear, as I can see no other explanation. My daughter and I, who live in Germany, were visiting my father who lives in UK.

We had just returned from a car journey and then my father gave me a crumpled piece of paper. He told me it might be important as it had our family names on it. He told me he had found it uncrumpled under my car seat, had thought of throwing it away, crumpled it, then changed his mind and gave it to me.

I looked at it and saw that it was an accommodation receipt at Sai Baba's ashram in India for my daughter, her brother and their Mother. It was dated from August 2016 and we were now in October 2016. I had not been staying with them and was in Germany at the time

It was only valid for their first ten days, and actually became useless when that part was over. They had then had to get another receipt for their subsequent period of stay.

So how had a useless two-month-old Indian receipt been found under the seat of my Dad's car in UK? You might suggest from my daughter. Well she assured me she had no recollection of this receipt. Moreover, when I picked her up from her Mother's, I had packed all her clothes from my home. The clothes she had on were a brand new coat, on its first time of wearing and some very tight jeans.

So, there was no way she could have kept that receipt in her trousers to be discovered by my Father uncrumpled and unfolded. And what would be the point in her carefully placing a two-month-old useless receipt there? She was seven at the time.

I like to think it was placed there by Sai Baba - why I don't know.

The accommodation slip that just appeared from nowhere (names obscured)

Butterfly Fly By

I was sitting on the bank of a river in a secluded spot in south India, meditating. I was just thinking about someone recounting how when a butterfly landed between his eyebrows, he then gained enlightenment. A cute tale.

But the second I recalled this, a butterfly landed between my eyes! And such an event never happened before or since. By the way I did not get enlightenment that time (!), I was simply very wonderstruck.

Disappearance of a Ring

I have a copper bowl which I use to carry out the *Agnihotra* ritual. I would often pick it by its holding rings on either side while the fire was still burning and hold it near me. This was a little dangerous, but I believed I was careful.

Then one morning I saw one of the rings was missing - and I have never found it. The ring is solid copper, and 4cm in diameter.

How can a solid ring become detached and just disappear? Maybe it was done as protection as my Master was not happy that I was taking the fire so near me. He could foresee that one day an accident would happen and has prevented this.

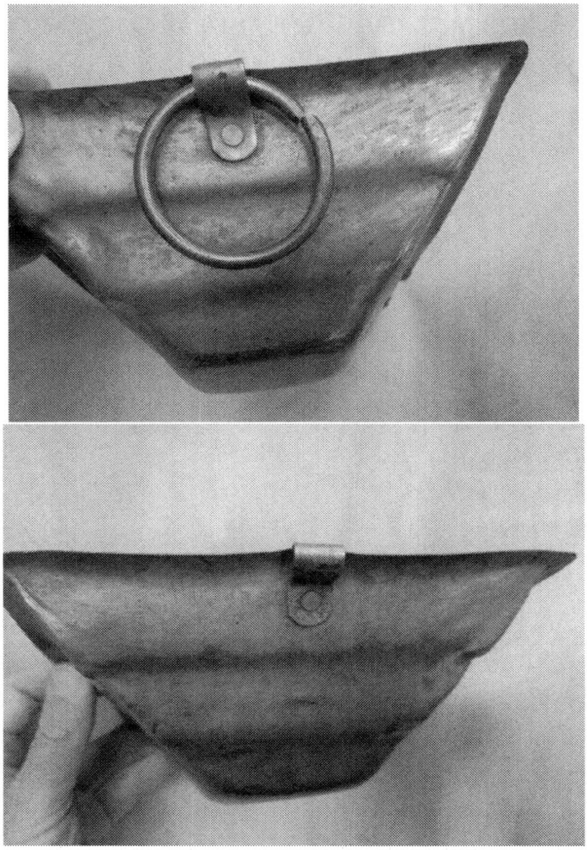

The copper dish with vanished ring on one side

Easter Gift

I was walking with my daughter in the main park. It was Easter Sunday and we had just been to church and had a very joyful time. Then she suddenly gasped and bent down on the grass picking up a small object. She showed it to me in wonderment. It was a crucifix, made of some alloy and it has been treasured ever since.

The crucifix found on Easter Sunday

Cross Confirmation

I wonder if you know the book *A Course in Miracles*. This book has transformed the lives of many people since it came out in the 1970's and its teachings powerfully echo around the world. I had been studying it and finding so many eureka moments that I was continually amazed at how the book told me just what I needed to know. I was making unheard of important positive shifts in my thinking and behaviour.

There was one evening when I was just dumbfounded at its wisdom, as I had a wonderfully profound insight into a self-imposed limiting belief. This new awareness joyfully stayed with me throughout the evening until I went to sleep.

The next morning, I opened my front door and I found a cross hanging on the handle. It was made of wood with woven threads around it. I was amazed as *A Course in Miracles* has a deeply Christian message and I felt the cross was connected with my miraculous evening.

I was filled with joy at its appearance. But I wanted it confirmed and so I wrote to Benjamin Creme, the great English spiritual teacher, who told me that Jesus had left it on my door as a sign of His blessing.

The cross gift

By the way, I have been helped profusely by Benjamin Creme since I was twenty. I have gained so much solace and knowledge from his work broadcasting the fact of Lord Maitreya and the Masters in the world. I also practised Transmission Meditation, which he founded, for many years and found it immensely rewarding.

I actually have hundreds of events connected with the above, but they are all personal and subjective, so outside the scope of this book. Thank you, Mr Creme!

Cool Penny

When I became heavily interested in spirituality at 18, my Mother gave me an old silver penny that had been given to her by her Father. He wanted me to have it. She told me that he had instructed that whenever I needed emotional support, I was to rub the penny and think of him. Then I would feel a cool sensation and spiritual support would be sent me. This penny had a hole in it and I could wear it on a chain.

I had occasion many times to ask for help using the penny. Then I would feel this strange otherworldly cold sensation, accompanied by a feeling of upliftment. This was a source of great help to me, before I became a follower of Sathya Sai Baba and then did not need it anymore.

Cricket Bat Luck

I was in the school playground with my friends and next to us were some older boys playing with a cricket bat and tennis ball. By accident I got too close to them and one big lad swung round with full force and the bat hit me on the chin. But I did not feel anything at all. I was amazed and I can recall staring at my leg in disbelief. I told my parents about it and I can remember it happening to this day.

Childlike Inspiration

While writing another book, there were plenty of helpful coincidences. One such happened like this:

I had written about the quality of childlike purity and how this can be rediscovered through spirituality. Then I joined my reading of *I am That,* one of the books I was referring to for inspiration and quotes. The very next line where I was up to Nisargadatta Maharaj said,

“I am now 74, yet feel as if I am an infant. I feel in spite of all the changes I am a child. My Guru told me that a child, which is you even now, is your real Self. Go back to your pure being where I AM is still in its purity, before it got contaminated with ‘this I am’ or ‘that I am’”.

So that quote went in the book as support from a great teacher, about how we are all in essence, as the inner self, pure, childlike and innocent. If you don't believe me, live a good helpful life, meditate and find this within you.

Flat Choice

I had been given a letter to deliver to someone I did not know. I went to the building given on the address, but then found that there were no clues as to who lived where. It was a large block of flats with five floors, each floor opening out to six apartments.

So instead of asking someone where this person lived, I thought I would trust guidance and intuition. I asked within and received the answer to go to the third floor... and when I was there, I was prompted to knock on a particular door. It was the right one!

Wonder Bus

I had been staying for some time in 2003 with my friend Visvanathan at his charming and inspirational community home Aum Pranava ashram in Tamil Nadu, India. There were ample opportunities to help out and one way was to go shopping in the local town. This was situated 15 minutes drive away, so I would regularly hop on the moped and buy provisions.

One afternoon I was just coming to a stop at a rather busy intersection coming into the town of Tenkasi, when a medium sized private bus went past me.

It certainly caught my eye as on the side was written in large letters D'ALBI TRAVELS. To find my surname in south India was a big shock to say the least.

And as I watched wonderstruck as the bus went past me, there on the back door was written my full name D'ALBI MARK. Ok it actually said D'ALBI MARKETING, but that almost counts.

I have found by internet search a few D'Albis in the world, but that was the only time I heard of it in India - when my name actually went right past me on a bus!

Colour Sense

In my late 20's I trained with an esoteric group. Part of the course was to become more aware of subtle vibrations and one such exercise involved us putting on a blindfold.

We were then handed differently brightly coloured scarves to see if we could sense the change in colour through our fingers. And though I cannot recall guessing the correct colour, I certainly did feel a change in their 'vibration' as I held each in turn and so did the other participants. We could actually feel the colours!

Confused Muddle Couple

I was with a friend in Thailand and we were organising visas from the Indian embassy to go back to India. The official told us we were the last ones to receive long term visas, which was fortunate in itself. He told us to come back in a week to pick up our stamped passports.

So we went to a beach and enjoyed the seaside. Then we came back to Bangkok and the first evening were looking round some shops. I suddenly noticed that two clocks were stating the wrong day – two! They said Monday, but it was Tuesday.

I asked someone and but they confirmed to my shock it was in fact Monday. We had both made a mistake with what day it was and had arrived one day earlier than we planned. Oh well, that was pretty dumb!

Then we went and sorted out the visas. But an unforeseen problem transpired and my friend went into panic mode, as it would take her a few days to fix. Our flights were booked in two days costing thousands of dollars!

By a miracle she managed to procure the documents in one day and so we could fly out with no time to spare. But without that extra day that our 'mistake' had given us, we would have missed our flights and been in dire financial problems.

I think we were helped to be so muddled up, because the confusion up ahead had been foreseen by angelic help.

Batman's Friends

While living in India someone gave me the Batman movie to see. After seeing it I went outside and there on the pavement outside the flat was a dead bat. Quite a coincidence as I had never seen one before.

Then the year later someone gave me the next Batman video. The evening after seeing it, a bat invaded our flat and started flying around inside. It would not leave and it took maybe 20 minutes to before it would leave. That was a one-off event.

Sure, there are bats in India, but can they tell when I watch movies about them?

Mysterious Meetings

Pink for Love

My first sight of subtle energy came as quite a surprise. I was 19 at the time and I was with an old lady who was talking about her dead husband. She had tears in her eyes and was rather emotional as she recalled him fondly.

Suddenly, and to me very oddly, a halo of strong pink hue appeared above her head. It was a few inches wide and stayed there for a few minutes. I just let her talk and pondered on this beautiful light above her head. It is something I can never forget.

Gold for Wisdom

Then a couple of months later I was at a Buddhist meditation class. There was an old Burmese master there teaching us. His name was U Nyanika. He was 80 years old, but was very fit and could briskly walk up the stairs. He liked me and once asked me to meditate with him and gave me some good advice.

One evening, as he spoke to the group, there appeared a golden halo shining above his head. It was very beautiful and I felt overjoyed looking at it. He was the first 'holy person' that I met.

What goes Down must Come Up!

It was the day before I was to leave for some months abroad in India. I was speaking with someone in my family. Then next to her appearing in the air for some 30 seconds, was a black line in the form of a proportionately drawn deep curve, about 30 cm in depth.

I was mystified and wondered if something was wrong with my eyes. Then a couple of hours later I was talking with another family member - you guessed it, the same deep curved line appeared next to him, hanging in the air for a minute!

I was totally perplexed and remained so, until a year or so later. Then I realised it referred to what was going to happen to these two people in my family.

At the time of appearing the graph-like line showed they were both going to go right down; their lives would deteriorate, but after some time they would come back up again and their lives would improve and come back to normal.

This indeed is what happened and I realised the lines were a graph, depicting their down and up fortunes.

Rosy Show

Only once have I seen the complete emotional body aura of someone. This was during a meditation and the guy in front of me had a beautiful rich rosy colour all around 'him'.

Why I put *him* in inverted commas is because we are more properly our auric emanations and not the physical body. The physical body is our vehicle in this world, and our aura is the light-vibration of our mental and emotional life.

The true Self, the Atma, is that which radiates eternally as pure consciousness. This is who we really are and everything happens 'in us'.

Otherwise, I have seen parts of people's auras hundreds of times, in different colours. I have also seen the edge of the vital auric body that stretches around the physical body with a border like a black line. Its distance from the physical body varies in accordance with the amount of vitality the person has.

Pedal Protection

My work these days involves travelling to various clients as a community psychiatric nurse. Sometimes I walk, or take public transport, but I also use a bicycle.

After seeing one client, as I was getting on my bike a clear intuitive thought came to me, "There is danger on the way to the next client." Well, I received this thought with some surprise - it was not as if I had thought it, it came from an outside source.

But I set off as usual and the way led along a wide pavement meaning that I could go quite fast. There was just one woman ahead, walking towards me. About 50 metres away I diverted my path slightly so we would not collide.

But then she seemed to be matching her direction to mine and as I changed, so she changed with me so that I had to slow down quite a bit. As I passed her, I said "sorry" as she might have thought I should have avoided her better. She was smiling at me as I went by, which in itself was strange. This all took five seconds and then I was past her and I pushed the pedals faster to gain speed.

There was just one man ahead walking in the same direction, obviously with his back to me. I went to pass him with maybe one metre distance, but just as I was alongside him, he suddenly without looking around, made a right angle turn and veered towards me, narrowly missing me.

I was shocked and looked back to see him walking and then stopping and then changing his direction again. He did not seem of right mind.

So, I firmly believe that I received through intuition or angelic help, information forewarning me of the danger ahead. I also think the lady was there to make me slow down and she made me lose 50% of the speed I had. As I went past the man, I had a narrow escape. A collision would have been very dangerous.

Thursdays are Special Days

My Guru Sathya Sai Baba has directed His followers to keep Thursdays as a day of divine worship, singing, service and chanting. Many times, I have felt specially blessed by Him on Thursdays, especially when I was at work in hospital. I could feel His sweet Presence with me to a profound level of support and comfort.

On one particular Thursday I was travelling back from a hospital shift. I stepped onto an underground train and stood in the central area. Then a travelling busker band walked on next to me.

They had a guitar, double bass(!), banjo and looked hippyish. We had an amusing interchange about them not wanting to begin playing as they might be caught by officials as the doors were still open.

Then they amazingly began their set with three tuneful “Oms”. I could not believe it! If I had not been working, I would have been attending the Sai Baba *Bhajan* session of spiritual songs and we would have chanted 3 Oms at the beginning!

I really enjoyed their music and then I had to change trains. I sat down in the compartment and next to me was a young American couple who were talking at length and quite deeply about going on spiritual retreats. Wow the second spiritual experience in ten minutes!

Then as I journeyed on, I thought to myself ‘I am sure there is one more experience to come, to make it up to the magic three’!

The last leg of the journey was underway and the only chance for this to happen seemed to be a couple of young women who were talking just opposite me.

I strained my ears to hear what they were saying for the next 15 minutes. And lo and behold, in their last conversation before I had to disembark, one woman started to talk about her habit of meditation, how it did her good and how she would wake up early to practise it.

These three experiences on one Thursday made me feel ecstatic. I felt the spiritual world was very near me and Sai Baba was watching over me. I felt my inner connection strengthened and I had renewed vigour to carry on through all the mundanity and routine. It was wonderful support on the spiritual path.

Aid in Need

I had a disturbing encounter while working on a psychiatric ward. Afterwards I was travelling back on public transport and I noticed a young woman looking at me quite a lot.

Then we disembarked at the same station and seemed to go separate ways. But then 30 seconds later she came up to me and asked me for some directions smiling very intently at me. I noticed her blue eyes were warm and full of affection. So, I told her and then went on my way, feeling quite uplifted now.

I believe she was sent my way to cheer me up.

Fun Confirmation

My path to start working in Germany was a long one, which included learning the language and then retraining in my professional job. After finishing my training and gaining my first employment, I was travelling to my first placement on the train.

Beforehand that day I had prayed to the Masters to give me a sign. I know this was selfish and they have better things to do, but I was so excited to work again after five years.

So, I was sitting on the train and I saw that a young man seated on the same side, was turning his head looking at me for quite some time. This left me feeling a little disconcerted.

Then after two or three stops he stood up to leave and as he passed me, he looked at me and said “Viel spass”, which means ‘have fun’ in German. Then I realised this was the sign I had asked for!

It was very kind of him to take the trouble, but I do feel bad about wasting his time.

With a Wave of Her Hand

I was travelling to work on a tram. Everything seemed ordinary enough. But then the lady opposite me looked upwards and moved her hand slowly in the air, exactly like Sai Baba. She did this for maybe 15 seconds, which is a long time to do something that was pretty strange and in plain sight of other people on a tram.

She was maybe in her mid-thirties, nicely dressed with shortish hair. I was looking at her slightly surreptitiously, as it is not right to stare at someone full-on. There was another man behind her, also looking on curiously.

For those who do not know, Sai Baba would perform this gesture regularly. Only he has been known to act in this way and the lady demonstrated a perfect likeness. He said of this action that He was communicating with unseen beings.

Seeing the Blind

One afternoon I was with my daughter and we were walking along a station platform and talking about what privations blind people suffer.

At that moment we turned a corner and a blind man walked past us with a stick. We both remarked on what a wonderful coincidence this was!

All Knowing Penniless Wanderer

I was with my good friend Visvanathan. I was on the back of his motorbike and we were exploring the countryside some distance from Aum Pranava Ashram, his community that helps destitute children and homeless old people.

Visvanathan likes to stop and give money to poor homeless wanderers that he meets along the way. So, he pulled up next to this old man who was dressed in old dirty clothes and had a stick. The two of them were then engaged in conversation for some five minutes.

Then he translated his last sentence to me, which was: ‘Say something about him (me)’, the old man looked at me and said ‘Sri Lanka, visa.’ Visvanathan looked very happy and I was surprised at the old man’s words.

After they finished speaking Visvanathan was very joyful as he recounted that the old man was a seer and had told him many private details about himself. When asked about me he had indeed confirmed exactly what I was about to do in two weeks: fly to Sri Lanka to arrange a new visa. Amazing!

After a few years, Visvanathan found out the old man's name was Iyakkiadum Perumal Swami. He was a saint and his shrine is in Shenkottai, Tamil Nadu.

Iyakkiadum Perumal Swami

Irritated by a Goddess

While staying with my aforementioned friend Visvanathan, I was inspired by the idea to go on a pilgrimage to Meenakshi Temple, in Madurai, which was some four hours away.

The Goddess Meenakshi is a young woman, famed in legends for marrying Lord Shiva and her temple is very large. When I brought up my plan to Visvanathan, he seemed to go into a trance. I could see some white light around his head and the atmosphere became enhanced. He then said, "Because you are going just to see Meenakshi, she will come and see you. But you will get irritated with her."

I am well used to the fact of the Masters and Saints blessing people with their physical or subtle presence, to comfort, heal or ward off danger and most often in disguise. So I was more than hoping that this would turn out to be true. I suspected that Meenakshi would disguise herself as a beggar. But it was intriguing! How could I get irritated in the presence of a Goddess?

So, on reaching the temple, I kept a close look out at the beggars, hoping that I could see her. Soon I was lost in the grandeur, mystery and sacred ambience of the temple. It is very large with many different areas and always full of devotees. I wandered into what seemed to be an exhibition room, with panels describing the history of the temple.

A young student approached me with a clipboard and asked me if she could pose some questions. I somewhat reluctantly accepted and she then began with her survey. I can only recall one question, which was 'what would I suggest as an improvement?' I told her that foreigners should be allowed entrance into the inner sanctum, which was only allowed for Hindus.

Then after some time I felt that was enough questions and I wanted to go. There was a middle-aged lady standing there, who had been staring at me the whole time during the questionnaire. I felt irritated and told her 'please don't stare as it is rude'.

The young lady then told me, 'Don't worry this is my Mother.' I felt embarrassed and apologised and then we ended the interview.

Off I went, glad to have this over and done with and went on walking around the temple. After five minutes I suddenly thought: could this have been Meenakshi? Meenakshi is a young lady - and I became annoyed with her. Oh no!

I rushed back to the hall, and searched in the environs, but she was nowhere to be seen. Well, it was all Her Leela!

Meenakshi as traditionally depicted

Destiny Changes by a Train Encounter

It was 2004 and I had been living at the ashram of my beloved teacher, Sathya Sai Baba. For some 18 months I had been working in one of the canteens. It was very enjoyable work, but somehow, I felt I needed more of a career challenge. As there seemed no other work available in the ashram, I was planning to leave in the next two weeks.

Then, while travelling back from my friend Visvanathan, I had a life changing experience. The train journey was long so I had gone for a wander through the carriage. I saw a monk who I recognised as accompanying Amritanandamayi Ma and I stopped to pay my respects to him.

He and the other passengers kindly asked me to sit with them and we chatted away, as people do in India. I told them where I was living and one of the passengers told me:

"My name is Professor Rao and I used to work with Professor Roberts (name changed) at xyz institute *(place forgotten)*. He is now living at Sai Baba's ashram. Please will you remember me to him when you return." I readily agreed.

A day or two after my return to Prashanti Nilayam, Sai Baba's ashram, I saw Prof. Roberts getting out of a van in the ashram and so I went over to pass on the greetings of this Prof. Rao. Prof. Roberts was surprised as he did not know anyone by that name from that institution.

But then he became interested in me and asked me about myself. He invited me to visit him the next day at the location of his present job, which was head of a department in the ashram.

The next day I found myself being interviewed for a job by Prof. Roberts, which I accepted. I stayed there for the next six wonderful years and I was able to be very useful to them. I cannot adequately describe the joy I had working with such exemplary people and how happy the work made me.

Certainly, I believe that the train encounter with the mysterious Prof. Rao was arranged by Baba. If that had not occurred, I would have left the ashram and life would have been entirely different.

3 in 1

One day I had three unusual experiences. The first came about during a time of great stress, when I had written to someone saying that they only saw me as a projection. I wrote this word in capital letters in my email, while sitting down in a park. Then I carried on walking.

Two minutes later I passed a group in conversation and the guy furthest from me said “and then imagine if it is a double projection…” The rest was out of earshot.

I was immediately gripped by this sudden coincidence and found it fascinating. I reflected that sure we all have double projections. The other person sees us as a projection and we see them as another projection - between us grows the mixture of the two projections!

Later, on my way home I was reading *A Course In Miracles*, the inspiring book of great wisdom. It has a section of lessons and the one for that day was “I will not see myself as a victim of the world”.

It was very apposite, as that was just how I was feeling. So, endeavouring to be in the spirit of a student I was repeating the lesson to myself: “I will not see myself as a victim of the world”.

As I got off the train, there I saw the word ‘Victims’ emblazoned in big letters on somebody’s pullover. That was the second coincidence that startled me.

Then I arrived home and after a few minutes stepped into the shower. I started to imagine that the doorbell would go, but I would not bother to answer it and would simply carry on showering. After some moments this did indeed happen!

2 in 1

Yes, you guessed it, two incidents happened that day. I was travelling to work on the train and it was about 7:00. I was just relaxing and then I began to recall a medical problem concerning the wound of a patient I had dressed previously. I started to imagine this had caused a colleague to ring me to discuss it. As I was having this daydream, this indeed happened: I received the call and we discussed the problem!

After returning from work later that day, I was relaxing with a good book *The Sun Does Shine,* by Anthony Ray Hinton. He had been wrongly imprisoned on death row for 30 years and the book describes his time inside and how he rehabilitated himself upon release.

I imagined that if I was rich, I would invite him to stay for free in my home. Then I thought Richard Branson (a famous multi-millionaire British businessman) should invite him to his island home and pamper him to make up for all his misfortunes.

As I carried on reading, I found the author recounting just such a thing had happened. Sometime after gaining his freedom he had indeed been invited by Richard Branson to his island paradise and had met many celebrities!

Seven Years Ahead Sight

I was 33 years old and I was staying at the ashram of my beloved teacher Sathya Sai Baba. I was just coming out of the living quarters, when a stocky Indian man with a shaven head came up to me. I had never seen him before, but after a little small chat he proceeded to give me a warning:

"You know when you get to 40 you will lose everything. It will be a very challenging time for you." He spoke intensely and very seriously with total conviction and repeated his warning with concern.

I think I was a little bemused, and did not know what to think. But I had been unknowingly speaking with a great soul, for that is exactly what happened.

At 40 I lost my marriage, family, money, job, chosen country of residence, friends, ability to earn money, or speak with people. This happened as I had to uproot and move to a foreign country if I wanted to see my daughter.

And so, began years of difficulties, loneliness, isolation and relative poverty. I did indeed lose everything except my daughter and spiritual life.

Sai Baba was ever by my side giving me spiritual strength and I have always had great joy in being a Father.

Over the years, circumstances became slowly better, but it was a hard challenging time for me. I guess knowing it was all destined, as the Indian man told me, made it a tiny bit easier.

Muslim Yogi

When I was first in India, staying in Puttaparthi, the ashram of my Guru Sathya Sai Baba, I rented a hut in the village from a Muslim holy man. He had been the Iman of the local mosque and he had developed his own yogic powers.

He had shoulder length hair and he told me he could make his hair stand up using a specific mantra. I was intrigued, so he told me to visit him the next morning. And there he was with his hair standing up and bushy. It was quite a strange sight as you might imagine.

He also told me he could read my future. One of the things he told me is that I would lose all interest in the world after the age of 45. Well that has indeed come true! At 47, I suddenly gave up all contemporary media, such as the news or current affairs.

I had been up till then a news addict, spending one to two hours every day trawling through the stories. But I decided that passively taking in all the scandals, arguments, violence and criminal activity was just not healthy and lead to feelings of anxiety and helplessness. I realised I don’t need all that rubbish and I have not missed it since and fill my time with positive, healthy activities. Please try this yourself, you won’t look back!

Little Kritters

In my late 20’s I got to know a young lady and she invited me to her home. I made her acquaintance through a healer network and she was also a beautician. When we went into her lounge, I saw these little black creatures rushing to hide under her carpet!

They were not insects or anything physical. They had subtle energy bodies (!). I was aghast and asked her “What were those black creatures that ran away?” She said “Oh they live under the carpet, they were here before I came”, as if it was something normal! It was very strange and I’m thankful I’ve never seen such things again.

Sun Worshipper

I was in the ashram of Sathya Sai Baba, my wonderful Guru, and I saw someone engaged in some very startling behaviour. He was Indian, around 60, dressed like a sadhu, had shoulder length hair and he was staring at the sun.

He was standing with his head tilted up and gazing straight at it. I studied him for some time and as you might expect from this book, he kept on staring for some minutes. He was a sun-gazing yogi.

I approached him and he graciously consented to speak with me even though his English was very poor. He told me that he was getting energy from the sun and that the technique, as far as I could gather, was to look but not to see the sun.

Obviously, he had practised this technique deeply and had training from his guru, otherwise how he could do such a dangerous exercise. I saw him on a few other occasions practising this 'Sun worship' - he was always alone; it was not as if he did this for show, or to attract followers.

I have made research on the internet and there are people doing similar practices but only at dawn or sunset. Whereas this remarkable man was sungazing in full daylight.

Scar of Good Luck

I had the good fortune to meet with a young man who was a member of an erstwhile royal family of West Bengal, India. His family connections lead him to have privileged access to a great Yogi who was the Shankaracharya (bishop) of Jyothish Mutt, a monastery in the Himalayas. I was able to meet with the Shankaracharya, who was very friendly.

We went two or three times and one of the attendants spoke to my friend and I quite a bit. He even showed us a private view of the Yantra, a ceremonial artefact that had originally been used by Adi Shankaracharya hundreds of years ago and passed down the lineage of succession.

Then he told me something unusual and personal. He said that I had a scar on my inner thigh and that this signified I had spiritual power. Well ~~this~~ there is indeed a scar at that location. Of course, I had been wearing full length trousers and there was no way he could see this.

Broken Images

My princely friend, for that is what he would be had the royal family stayed in power, had an interest in Tantra. Not the popularised nonsense we have in the west, but an unusual branch practised by a few. Tantra means a method of enlightenment and there are many forms that it can take.

For his chosen tantric practice this young man liked to visit graveyards and carry out rituals there. He wanted me to come as well, but I refused.

But while we were speaking on this topic, a small mirror near us broke. Of course, this spooked us. And then on another day we were speaking on the same topic and a different mirror cracked!

Well that was enough to make me doubly scared - you won't catch me in a graveyard meditating.

Timely Advice

I was sitting on the subway, on my way on to have a very difficult conversation. I was feeling very disturbed and was worried that I might lose control and start becoming angry. I did not want that to happen, as it would be counterproductive. I started praying to my guru to help me to keep calm and I tried to remember His teachings and that He would send me help.

As the journey went on, I vaguely registered that opposite me was a young pretty lady. After a few stops, she took a book out of her bag and started reading. I noticed it was in English and the title was *Positive Moments*. I could tell it was a new age self-help type of book. Well that caught my attention, as here I was in Germany and it never happens that someone sits opposite me reading an English spiritual book.

This caught my attention even more as I had just been praying for help and maybe - just maybe - this was the help that had been sent. But I was too shy to begin talking to the lady while sitting on the crowded train. So, I kept quiet and told myself that I would speak to her if she left at my stop. And incredibly she did.

So, I plucked up courage while stepping onto the platform and asked her, "Excuse me, I could not help noticing you are reading a spiritual book and I was wondering if it might have a message for me? I am in a very stressful situation."

She took my request very calmly and replied, "Yes, I would like to help but I need to know the context of the situation you are in. Can you tell me something about it?"

I told her this was about confronting someone who I thought had been lying to me. She then answered, "This book teaches us that in difficult circumstances we should remember the positive moments you have had with the other person. Don't let the present situation make you forget other better times you may have had and bring those into the conversation."

I thanked her and told her that is just what I needed. I felt really buoyed up and cared for by my Guru. I followed the advice she gave me and it did indeed lead to a better interchange. I was able not to become irritated.

Light Transfer

I was working as a psychiatric nurse and I had just come back from a stay with my Guru, Sathya

Sai Baba. For much time after returning to UK I was filled with His spiritual joy. Of course, this was not something I would tell people about, it is personal.

One day I had to take the vital signs of an outpatient who seemed to be suffering from mild anxiety. As I took his pulse, I had to hold his wrist for a minute.

As I did so I could feel the blessing from Sai Baba entering this man's subtle energy body. But I said nothing as we were in a medical setting and I had just met him.

After taking his pulse he simply said, "Well, I don't need to be here", and walked out. It was an experience we both shared beyond words.

Hairdresser High

When I was 21, I stayed with Sathya Sai Baba for nine months. It was a time of incomparable bliss. When my time was over I had to come back to UK and get back to practical life. One thing I needed to do was have a haircut. So I went to a salon and the hairdresser set to work.

But around my head was the powerful energy blessing of Sai Baba. She began to feel this and not knowing why, started laughing with joy. Of course, how could I explain...it is all glory to Sai Baba.

Fragrant Attraction

I was staying a couple of weeks in Sri Lanka, as I needed to get a new visa to return to India. So, I was travelling around filling up the time and while staying in a guest house in Kandy, I met a friendly guy called David from Ireland. David had no interest in spirituality, but listened to my tales about Sai Baba.

As we were hanging out one evening in the lounge, I was telling David about Sai Baba sending me a fragrance from out of the ether.

In the middle of this story we both smelt jasmine! We were pretty surprised and after some moments of shock we started to hunt around for the source of its sudden appearance, as it was not going away.

But our search proved to be fruitless and it convinced the hitherto sceptic David so much that he made two or three visits to Sai Baba's ashram in the next few years. Good luck to you David!

Homely Find

I was 23 and I needed to find a place to stay in north London while I attended my psychiatric nursing course. I was from south London and I had no contact details for anyone in the area. So, I just opened up the yellow pages business listings under estate agents, closed my eyes, ran my finger along the entries and stopped at a particular one. I made an appointment and went there the next day and was shown a flat which I did not like.

After the viewing something told me to go for a walk and instead of going home I went in the opposite direction. After five minutes lo and behold I bumped into an old lady who I recognised from giving a talk at a Sai Baba meeting.

In the ensuing conversation I told her I was looking for a place and she told me she had a friend one street away who wanted a lodger. And that was where I stayed the next two years!

Staring Sadhu

I had gone to visit a well-known *hatha yogi* with my friend, Visvanathan. We had to climb up some way in the hills and then came across the yogi with a few followers.

We then had some chit chat and I noticed the yogi was giving me a lot of attention, speaking to me and looking at me, almost staring.

During our time there and for a few minutes I began to feel quite strange as if I could not think properly. I could not formulate thoughts normally and my mind was rather blank.

After about half an hour we left and on the way down I mentioned my confused state of mind to my friend. “He was trying to make you his disciple by saying some mantras on you,” was his explanation.

I was shocked and felt irritated, but as another yogi told me later, he did not succeed so why worry.

UNited Disharmony

When I was 18, I went to India for the first time to an international conference of young people, hosted by the United Nations of Youth, (not a UN body). We had the vision to create an organisation of young people to make the world a better place.

There were about 50 participants and it was held at Nainital, in the Himalayas. There were youth from all over the world and on occasions it proved difficult attaining this unity amongst us, especially regarding a common religious approach.

Unfortunately, there was an argument about coming together and chanting the OM. It was really silly.

But it upset the wonderful young lady from India whose job it was to host this idealistic gathering. This came to a climax at the ending ceremony and she could not take it anymore and left in tears.

There was some panic amongst us, but then a strong feeling took over me that I had to find her. I went quickly through the buildings and finally found her.

Some One inspired me to take her by the shoulders, look deeply in her eyes and tell her strongly "We need you".

I felt this strong current of lightfull energy course through me into her.

Well this had such a profound effect that she immediately relaxed, left her sorrows behind and composed herself to go back and finish the ceremony.

I must tell you this is totally unlike me. To clasp her and say those words was simply not me at all!

But after that she kept on looking at me with some sort of admiration. Even when we all went to her lovely home in Delhi, her family were also paying me a lot of close attention, as she must have told them about me.

But they were also very puzzled, as I did not appear special. I did not know what to say, so I did not mention the incident and nor did they. The energy transfer had nothing to do with me.

Thought Power Experiments

There was a period when I dabbled a bit practising thought power. I would try and make someone ahead of me turn around, simply by suggesting them to do so. And it worked many times. I have a friend Lucas who told me ~~he~~ people often stumble when he looks at them. It sounds crazy but he showed me it happening a few times.

Famous Psychic

I was travelling around India with a friend and a rather famous western spiritual teacher. We had many fascinating conversations with him and he regaled us with stories of his psychic experiences.

He told us he could see through matter and read minds. My friend challenged him to read his mind and this guy agreed that at some point later that day he would reveal what my friend had been thinking. The day went on and then after a couple of hours the psychic guy said "Oh you were thinking of suggesting we play cards". We were both amazed, as this was indeed his idea. And playing cards had never been mentioned between us before.

In regard to him seeing through things, once I was with him and he had to pick a token number out of a cloth bag. Number one (out of twenty others) gave the best option and of course he picked it.

Purple Robes

I was making a short journey from home, sitting at the back of a bus. Suddenly I sensed the atmosphere in the bus change, as if from a strong positive magnetic presence. I had never had this feeling before on public transport.

I looked up and saw a man taking his seat opposite me. He looked extraordinary. He only had one arm and was dressed in hippy purple flowing robes. He had a bag across his shoulders with a rainbow coloured strap.

I surreptitiously looked at him and was aware that he was looking at me. At one point he got out a CD from his bag and holding it started to turn his hand in circles in front of him, exactly as Sai Baba would do when materialising objects. What unusual behaviour!

After a short time, I had to get out at my stop, but I felt wonderfully and inexplicably rejuvenated. The rather dull feeling of loneliness I had been feeling was all gone. I have often wished to see him again, in which case I would definitely try and speak with him.

Street Psychic

In my early 20's I wanted to enter Sai Baba's university. Although it is held in very high regard in India, hardly any westerners have ever attended it. I was in Bangalore on my way to buy some books to study for the entrance exam. The streets were crowded and there was the odd tourist around as well, so me being there was hardly out of the ordinary.

I was just about to cross the street when a man started talking to me, trying to grab my attention. He certainly had it straight away, as he began by telling me I was trying to get into Sai Baba's university.

How did he know that? He almost had a kind of salesman's pitch about him, as he proceeded to try and impress me. He asked me if I wanted to know the name of my future wife and proceeded to write down two letters of a six-letter name down. Then he asked me for 100 rupees. I was a little annoyed at all this strange behaviour and made my way away from him fast. But for him to know what I was up to was nothing short of remarkable.

Nadi Palm Reader

India contains all sorts of wonderful things. One of them is the Nadi Palm readings. Tradition has it that hundreds of years ago a great yogi foresaw the futures of thousands of people and wrote these down on palm leaves.

People interested to know what is written about them can make an appointment with the palm leaf reader, who then takes out the correct palm leaf according to the date of your appointment with him.

So, I went along and had an interesting reading. He tells you about your past lives, which are of course unverifiable. He also related about the past of this life which was correct in some details.

For example, the length of time I was with my girlfriend in my twenties and also how old I was when I did a spiritual healing course. But his readings of the future have not come true - so far.

With a Wave of Their Hands

This account is one of my favourites. I had been praying to Sai Baba and He had filled me with much love, joy and bliss. I felt full to overflowing with His blessing and I felt inspired to walk along the main street and just let His Love shine out.

I had been walking some ten minutes and the pavement was quite crowded. Then unusually, a man passing me from the other direction, smiled at me as he went by, at the same time waving his hand downwards to the ground.

It is bit unusual when strangers meaningfully catch your eye, but to make a wave at the same time was doubly odd.

I walked on another minute... and then the same thing happened! This time a young woman smiled at me as she went by, and amazingly she also waved her hand at the ground!

I felt a bit disconcerted, but what to do. I carried on walking, pondering at this event. And then, yes you guessed it, another young man astoundingly did the same thing! Catching my eye as he went past with a smile and also waving at the ground.

Even now I feel very perplexed at this. It was as they knew I was shining with the love of Sai Baba and wanted to say hi. Who are these people? Are they always in such numbers on the streets? Or did they somehow contrive to be ready to sign to me as they went by separated by 100 metres?

Multiple Signs

One morning I received a much-awaited email from the Sai ashram with some very important welcome news. I was simply overjoyed and incredibly moved. They told me they would publish a book I had written. Wow this was one of the best things that had happened to me the last few years!

Then ten minutes later, someone from the Sai group who only rarely communicates, sent me some photos via social media of a Sai Baba event we just celebrated. That was like a confirmation of Grace.

Then ten minutes after that, as I was getting on a bus, a lady from the Sai Baba group was stepping off the bus and we greeted each other. That was another wow moment.

Then ten minutes after that I received notice of the cancellations of two clients who were next up on my list. That had never happened before. It meant I had 30 minutes free to just savour what had happened and meditate with joy on what had just happened.

Postscript

Dear reader, I pray that the Angels and Masters bless you and watch over you!

We are never without their help.

41623026R00042

Printed in Poland
by Amazon Fulfillment
Poland Sp. z o.o., Wrocław